AF588517

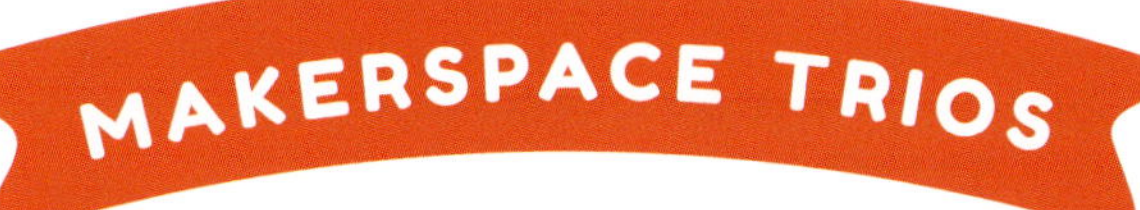

Creating with CARDBOARD, CRAYONS & DUCT TAPE

Rebecca Felix

Consulting Editor, Diane Craig,
M.A./Reading Specialist

Super Sandcastle

An Imprint of Abdo Publishing
abdobooks.com

abdobooks.com

Published by Abdo Publishing, a division of ABDO, PO Box 398166, Minneapolis, Minnesota 55439.

Printed in the United States of America, North Mankato, Minnesota
102021
012022

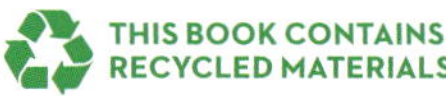
THIS BOOK CONTAINS RECYCLED MATERIALS

Design: Sarah DeYoung, Mighty Media, Inc.
Production: Mighty Media, Inc.
Editor: Megan Borgert-Spaniol
Cover Photographs: iStockphoto; Mighty Media, Inc.; Shutterstock Images
Interior Photographs: David Ingram/Flickr; iStockphoto; Jae C. Hong/AP Images; Littlelixie/Flickr; Mibrahim74/Wikimedia Commons; Michael Leavitt/Wikimedia Commons; Mighty Media, Inc.; Shutterstock Images; Slava Ostap/Wikimedia Commons

The following manufacturers/names appearing in this book are trademarks: Adidas®, ArtMinds™, Crayola®, Crocodile Crafts™, Crocs™, Duck Tape®, Elmer's®, Nike® Air Jordan

Library of Congress Control Number: 2021943030

Publisher's Cataloging-in-Publication Data
Names: Felix, Rebecca, author.
Title: Creating with cardboard, crayons & duct tape / by Rebecca Felix
Description: Minneapolis, Minnesota : Abdo Publishing, 2022 | Series: Makerspace trios | Includes online resources and index.
Identifiers: ISBN 9781532196409 (lib. bdg.) | ISBN 9781098218218 (ebook)
Subjects: LCSH: Handicraft--Juvenile literature. | Creative thinking--Juvenile literature. | Crayon drawing--Juvenile literature. | Cardboard sculpture--Juvenile literature. | Duct tape--Juvenile literature. | Mixed media crafts--Juvenile literature.
Classification: DDC 745.5--dc23

Super SandCastle™ books are created by a team of professional educators, reading specialists, and content developers around five essential components—phonemic awareness, phonics, vocabulary, text comprehension, and fluency—to assist young readers as they develop reading skills and strategies and increase their general knowledge. All books are written, reviewed, and leveled for guided reading and early reading intervention programs for use in shared, guided, and independent reading and writing activities to support a balanced approach to literacy instruction.

TO ADULT HELPERS

The projects in this book are fun and simple. There are just a few things to remember to keep kids safe. Some projects may use sharp or hot objects. Also, kids may be using messy supplies. Make sure they protect their clothes and work surfaces. Be ready to offer guidance during brainstorming and assist when necessary.

CONTENTS

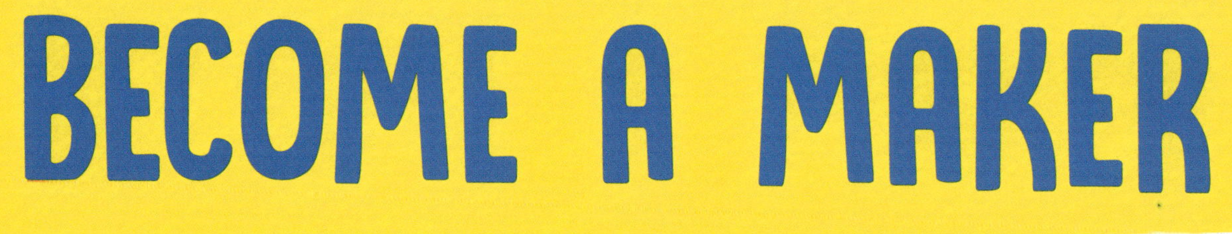

BECOME A MAKER

A makerspace is like a laboratory. It's a place where ideas are formed and problems are solved. Kids like you create amazing things in makerspaces. Many makerspaces are in schools and libraries. But they can also be in kitchens, bedrooms, and backyards. Anywhere can be a makerspace when you use imagination, inspiration, **collaboration**, and problem-solving!

Imagination

This takes you to new places and lets you experience new things. Anything is possible with imagination!

Inspiration

This is the spark that gives you an idea. Inspiration can come from almost anywhere!

Makerspace Toolbox

Collaboration

Makers work together. They ask questions and get ideas from everyone around them. Collaboration solves problems that seem impossible.

Problem-Solving

Things often don't go as planned when you're creating. But that's part of the fun! Find creative solutions to any problem that comes up. These will make your project even better.

EXPLORE CARDBOARD

You probably come across cardboard every day. It is a paper-based product used to box everything from mailed packages and furniture to crayons and cookies. Cardboard is also used to create signs, cartons, and much more.

Cardboard Properties

- Flexible
- Lightweight
- Stiff
- Sturdy

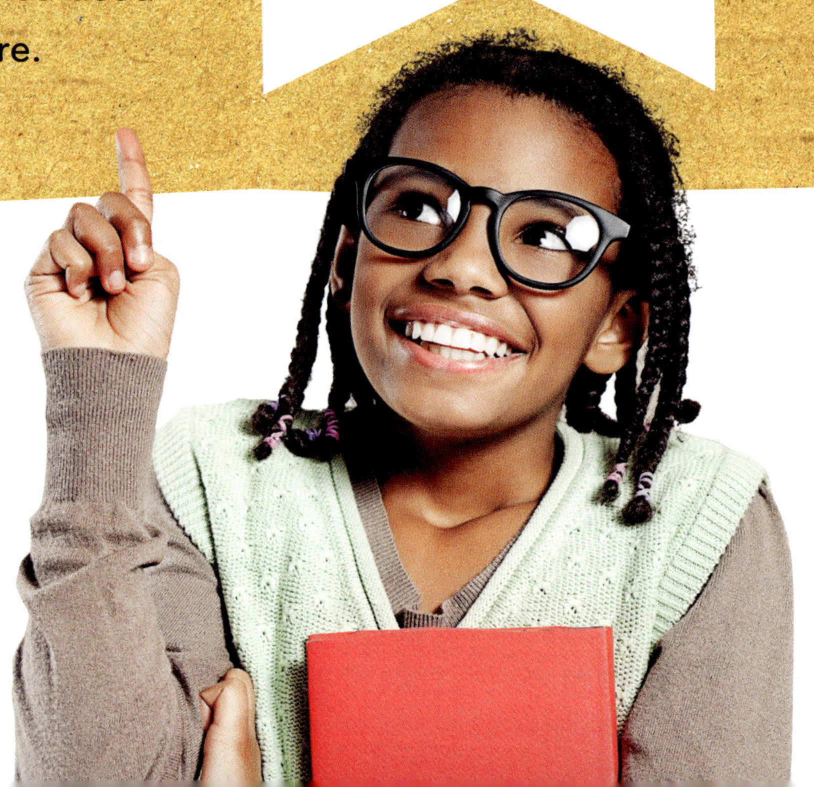

How Can You Use Cardboard?

Cardboard has many standard uses. But it can be used however you like in a makerspace! Let your imagination wander. What would it look like to use cardboard in a new way?

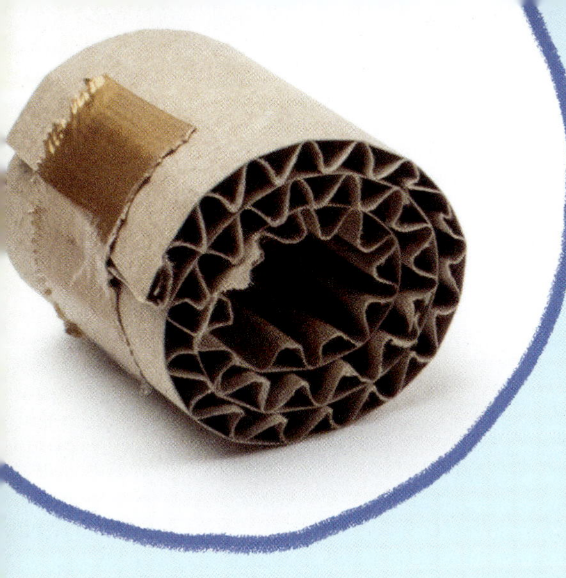

Cardboard as a Base

Could you stack pieces of it? Could you roll strips into a solid form?

Cardboard as Decoration

Could you make scales or feathers with it? Could you bend, cut, or tear it to create texture?

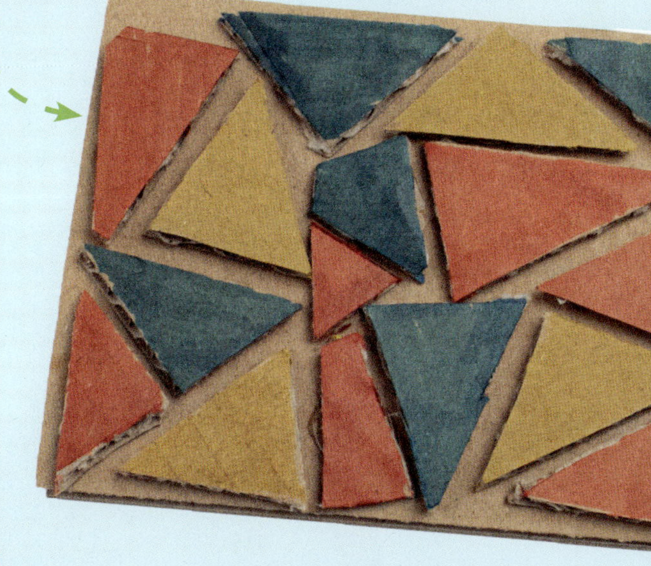

Cardboard as a Tool

Could you use it to prop up a project or hang an artwork?

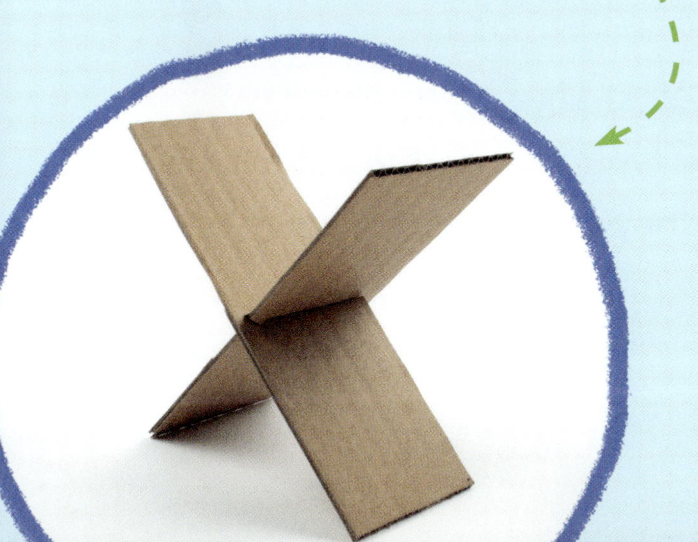

Cardboard Converted

Could you soak it in water or separate it into layers?

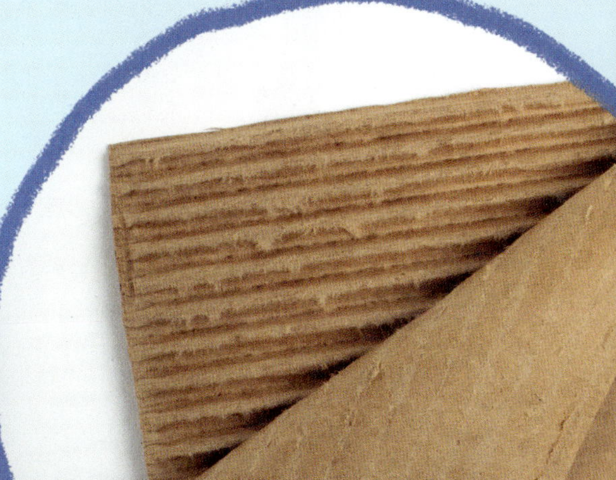

EXPLORE CRAYONS

Crayons are a common art supply. They are wax-based and come in many colors! People use crayons to draw, make signs, and more.

Crayon Properties

- Colorful
- Hard
- Pointed
- Waxy

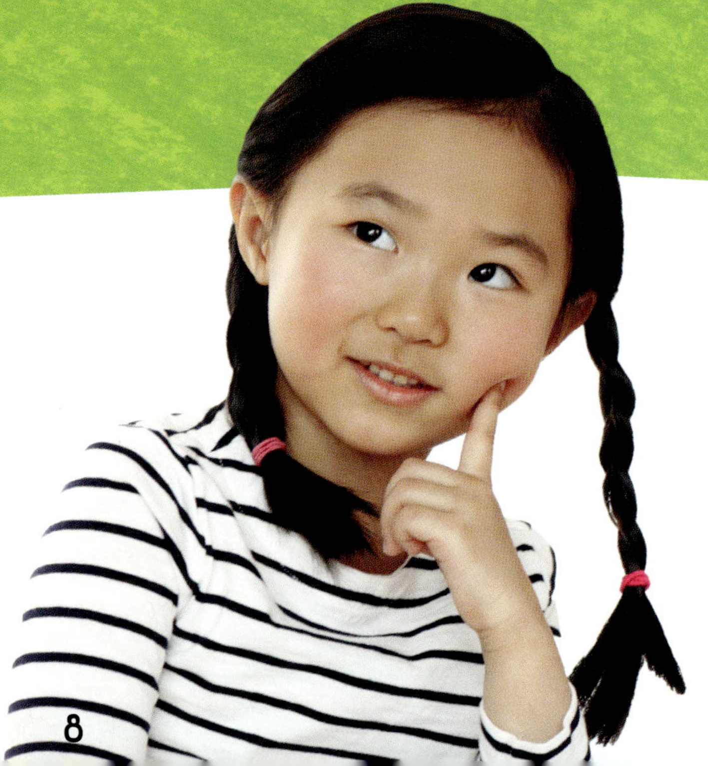

How Can You Use Crayons?

Crayons are typically used to color on paper. But they can be used however you like in a makerspace! Let your imagination wander. What would it look like to use crayons in a new way?

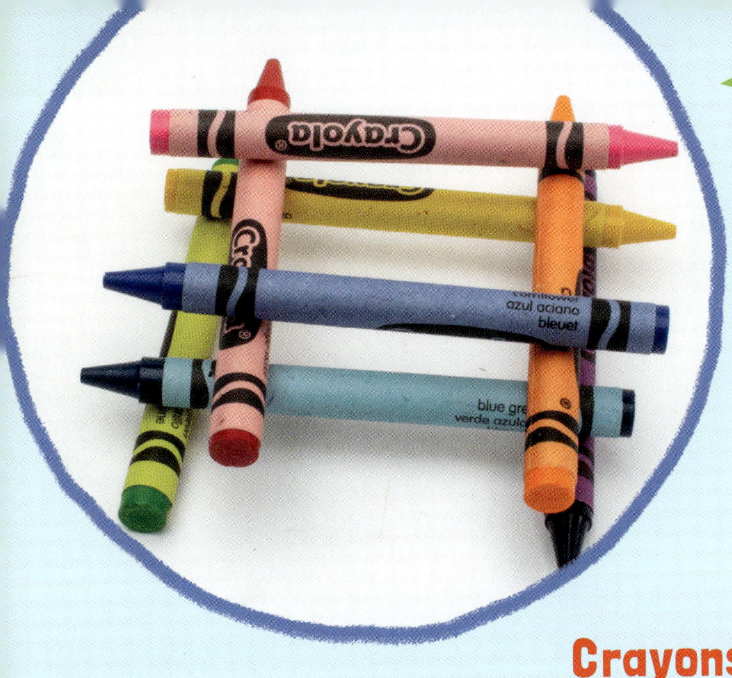

Crayons as a Base

Could you stack them into a tower or connect them into a solid wall?

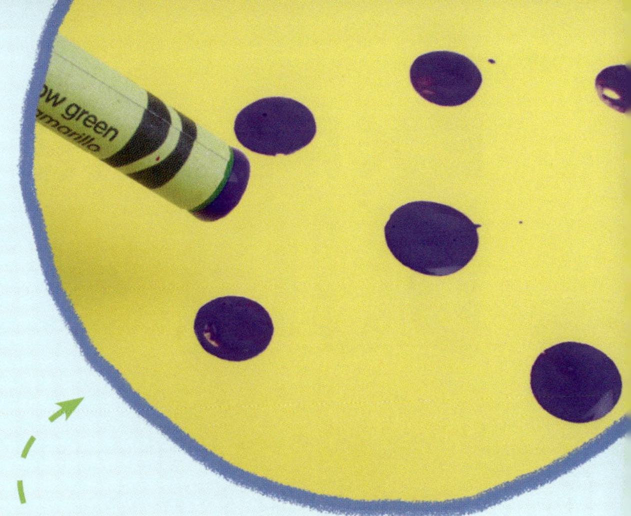

Crayons as a Tool

Could you use them as connecting pieces? Could you use their ends as stamps?

Crayons Converted

Could you melt them down? Could you peel off their paper covers and use those?

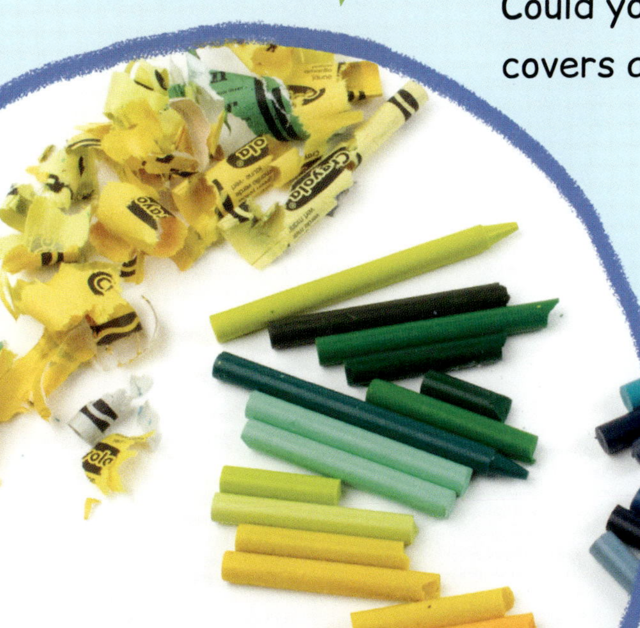

Crayons as Decoration

Could you cut them into confetti? Could you use them as spikes, eyebrows, or hair?

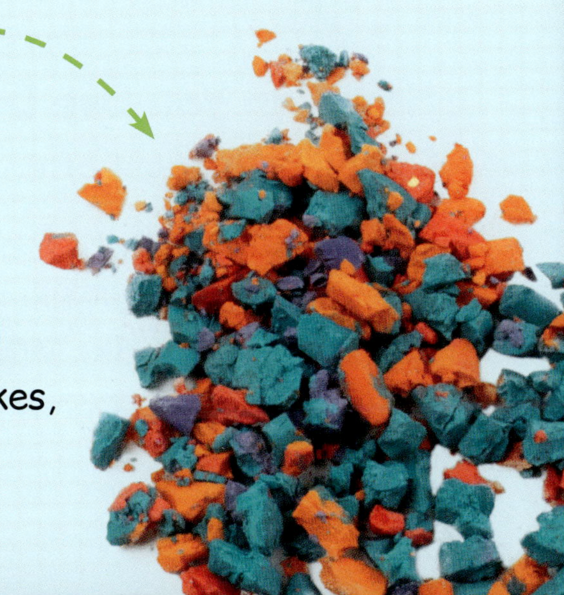

EXPLORE
DUCT TAPE

Have you ever used duct tape? It is a strong, sticky tape that comes in all kinds of colors. People use duct tape to repair cracks, leaks, and more. Many people also craft with duct tape!

Duct Tape Properties

- Bendable
- Sticky
- Strong
- Water-repellent

How Can You Use Duct Tape?

Duct tape is most often used to patch or fix things. But it can be used however you like in a makerspace! Let your imagination wander. What would it look like to use duct tape in a new way?

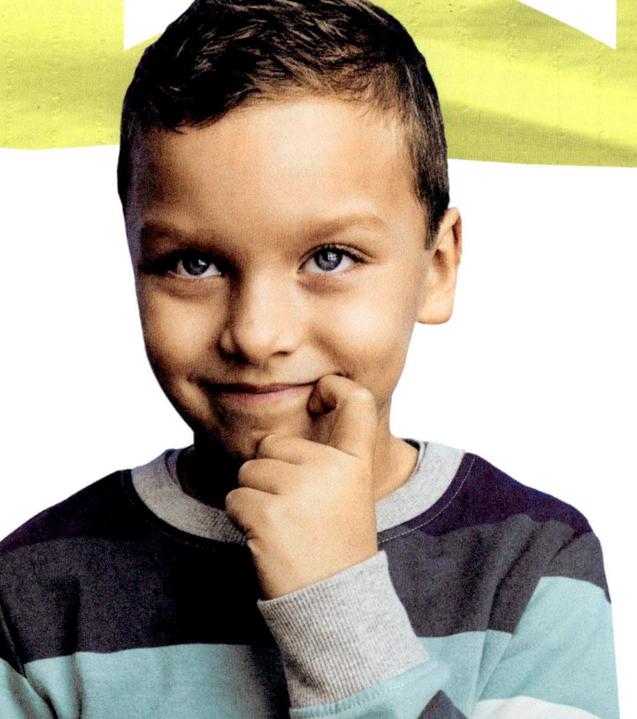

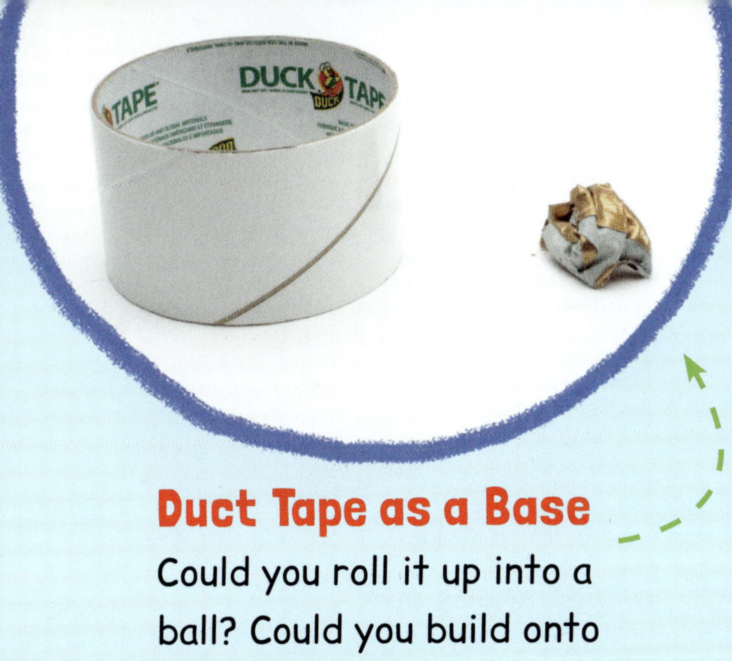

Duct Tape as a Base

Could you roll it up into a ball? Could you build onto an empty roll?

Duct Tape as a Tool

Could you make it into a handle or hanger?

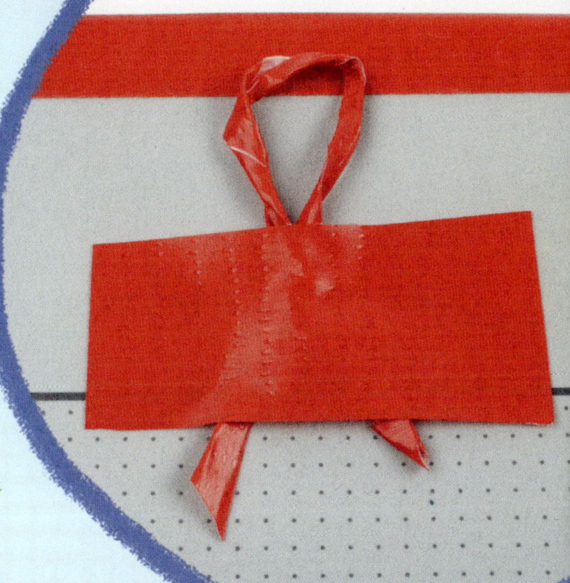

Duct Tape as Decoration

Could you fold it into strips and braid it?

Duct Tape Converted

Could you weave it or layer it into fabric?

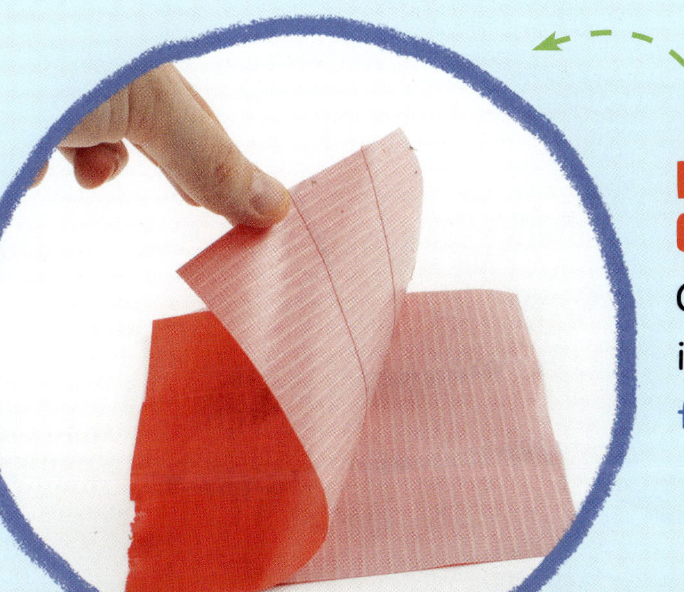

GET INSPIRED

People have used cardboard, crayons, and duct tape in all kinds of creative ways. Let these examples spark your imagination!

Artist Mike Leavitt makes replicas of popular shoes out of recycled cardboard. He has created cardboard Adidas, Crocs, Air Jordans, and more.

Athletes performing in the 2020 Summer Olympics in Japan slept on beds made with cardboard frames! Each bed could hold 440 pounds (200 kg).

Artist Herb Williams builds sculptures out of crayons. He has created artworks using hundreds of thousands of crayons.

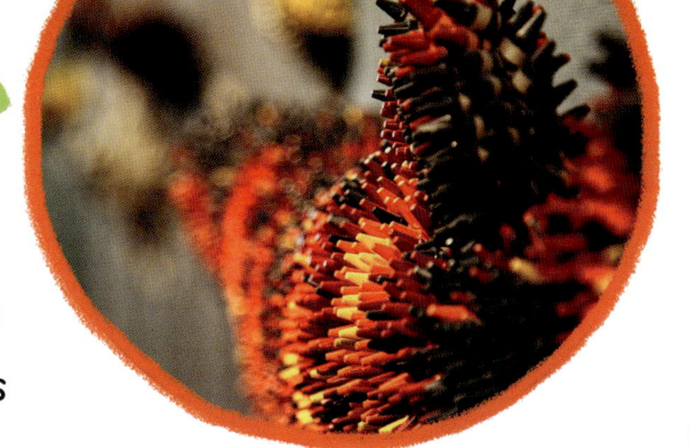

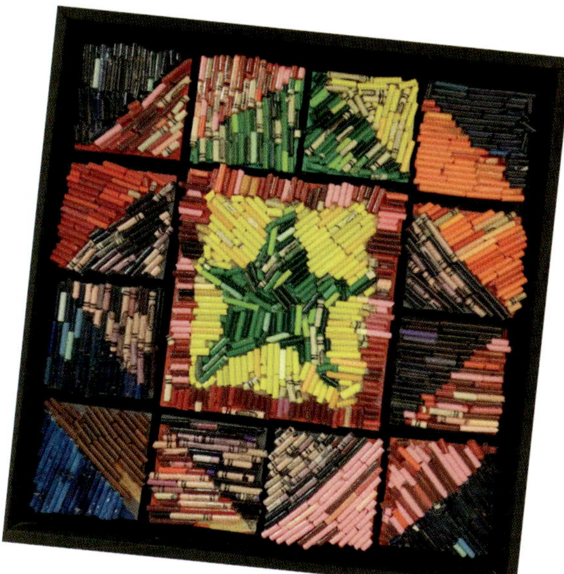

A dress made of colorful duct tape

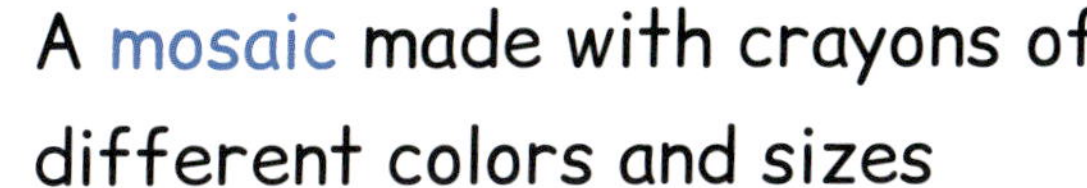

A mosaic made with crayons of different colors and sizes

Artist Slava Ostap made this tornado artwork using more than 400 rolls of duct tape!

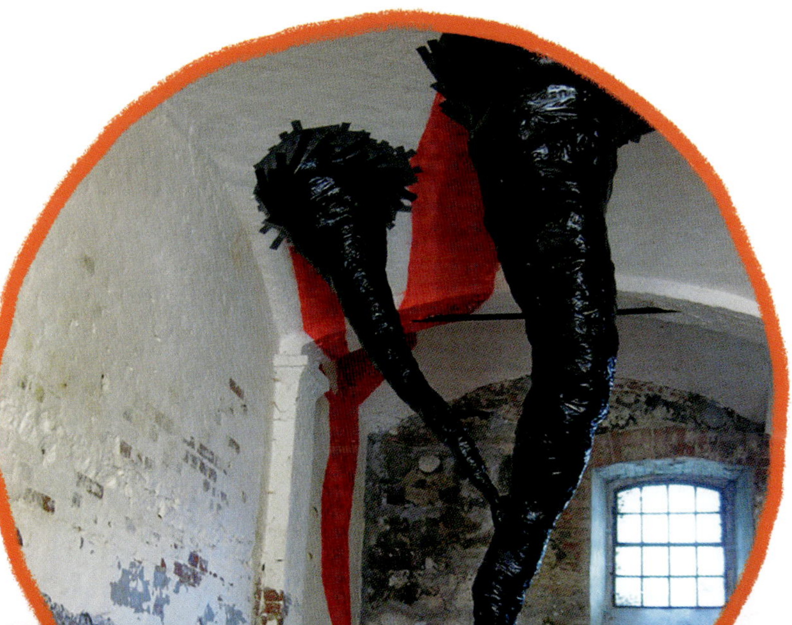

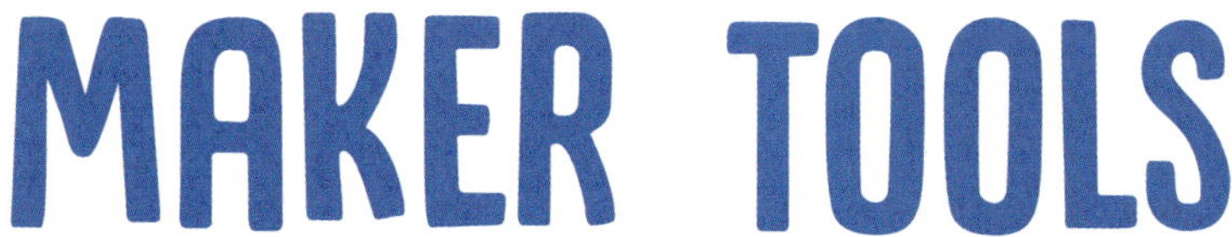

Are you inspired? Have you brainstormed some makerspace projects? It's time to gather your cardboard, crayons, and duct tape. You may also need a few everyday tools to cut and connect your primary materials.

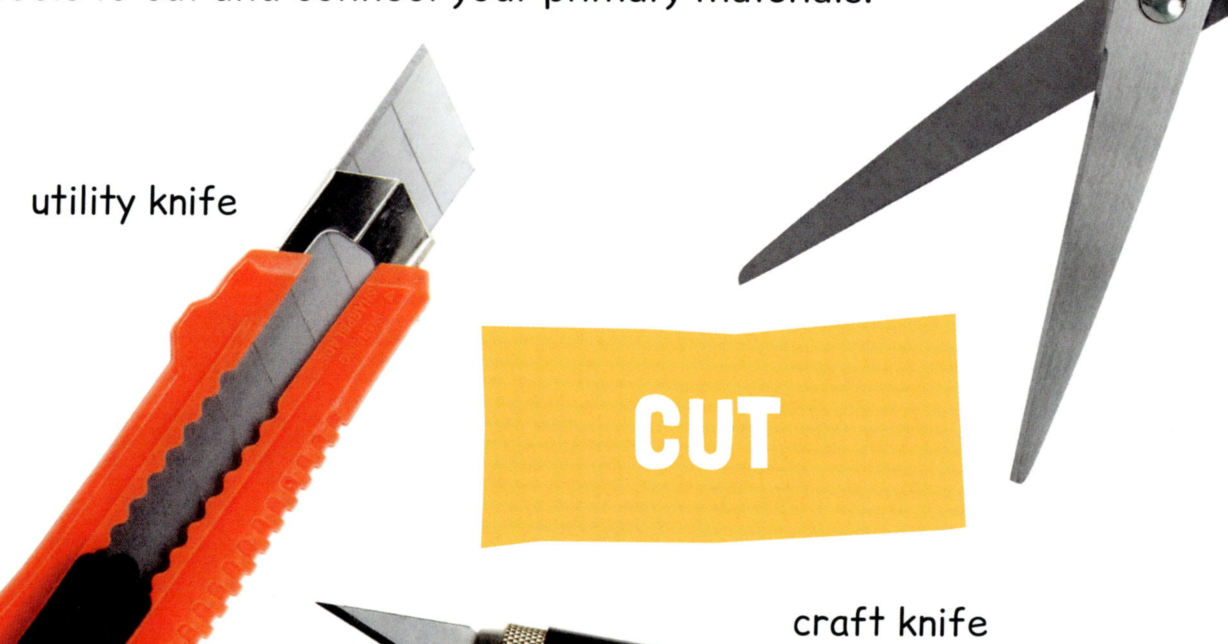

scissors

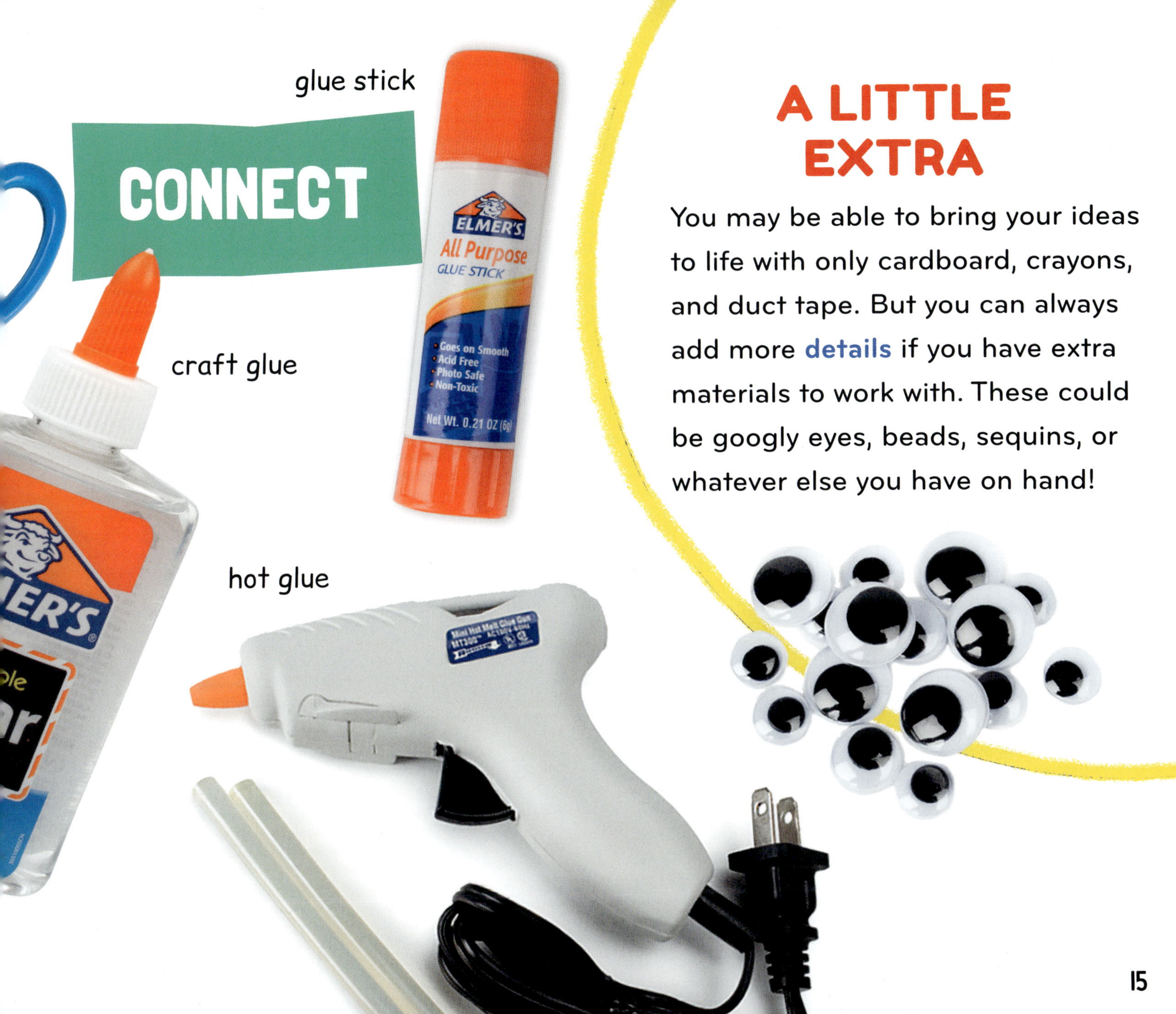

A LITTLE EXTRA

You may be able to bring your ideas to life with only cardboard, crayons, and duct tape. But you can always add more **details** if you have extra materials to work with. These could be googly eyes, beads, sequins, or whatever else you have on hand!

MAKING YOUR MAKERSPACE

You can let your imagination run wild in a makerspace. But be sure to follow these rules to stay safe and be respectful.

2 Be safe

Ask an adult for help when using sharp or hot tools, such as craft knives or glue guns.

1

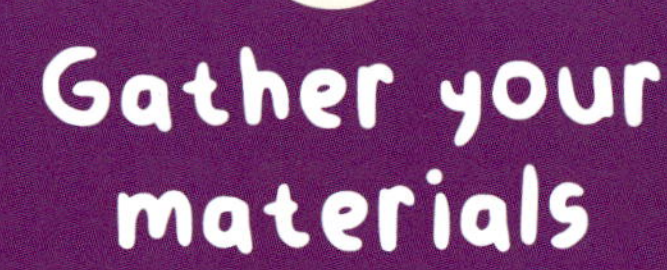

Make sure an adult says it's OK to use what you gather.

3 Share the space

Share supplies and space with other makers. You can invite them to share their ideas if you're feeling stuck!

4 Keep trying

Don't give up when things don't go exactly as planned. Instead, think about the problem you are having. What are some ways to solve it?

5 Clean up

Put away materials. Find a safe space to store unfinished projects until next time. And clean up any scraps, spills, or messes you made.

DISPLAY IT

Create an artwork from cardboard, crayons, and duct tape. Then put it on display!

A shoebox lid can become a painting frame.

Broken crayon pieces often get tossed aside. Find a fun way to make use of them.

You can melt crayons to create cool texture. Smash them into smaller bits so they melt more quickly. The bottom of a small jar or sturdy cup makes a good smashing tool.

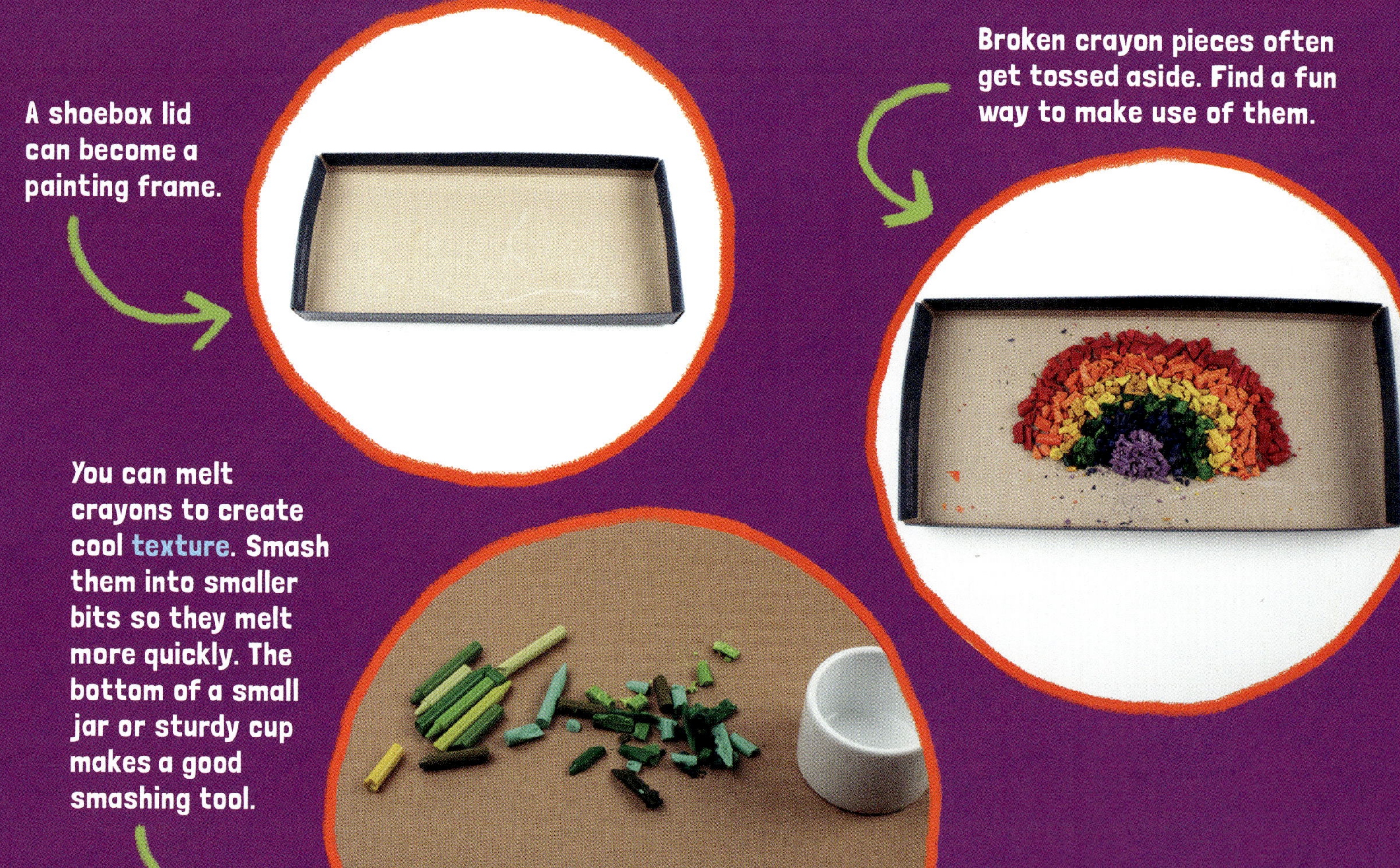

Use a hair dryer to melt your crayon bits. Or let them melt in the sun. Be patient!

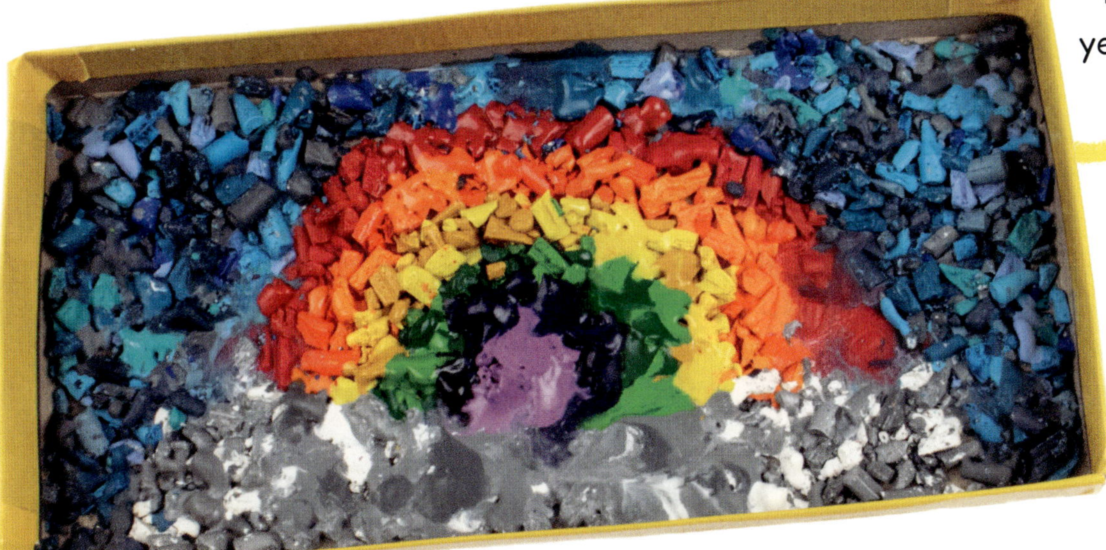

Duct tape adds a pop of color.

Imagine

Imagine ideas outside your own space and time. What might art look like in the year 3022? How might it be displayed?

Your Turn!

What artwork could you create from a cereal box or cardboard can?

Could you use the paper wrappings on crayons in a work of art?

Could full rolls of duct tape be turned into an art display?

WEAR IT

What wearable clothing or accessories could you make from cardboard, crayons, and duct tape?

Corrugated cardboard has a rippled layer. It makes for an interesting base for accessories!

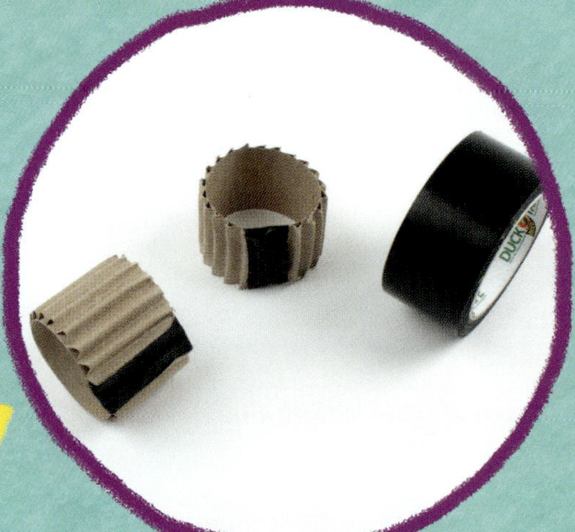

Crayons are fun decoration on a wristband. Strips of colorful duct tape can secure them to a cardboard duct-tape ring or a strip of corrugated cardboard.

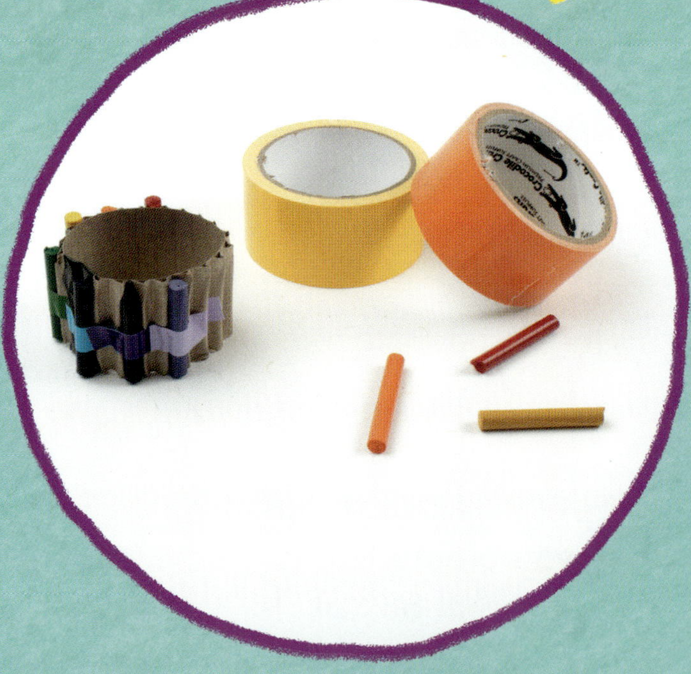

Finish your accessories with fun patterned duct tape!

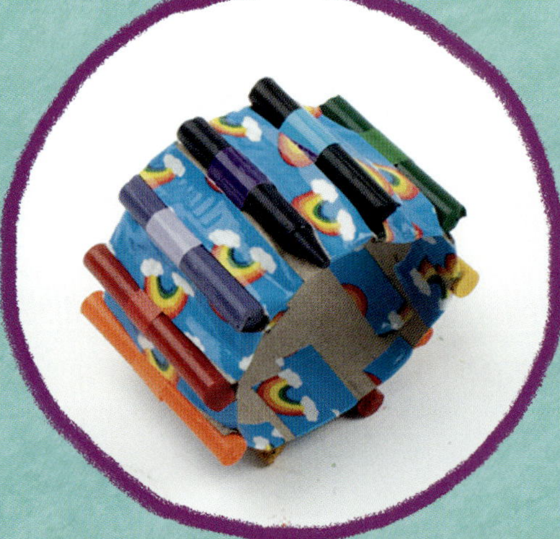

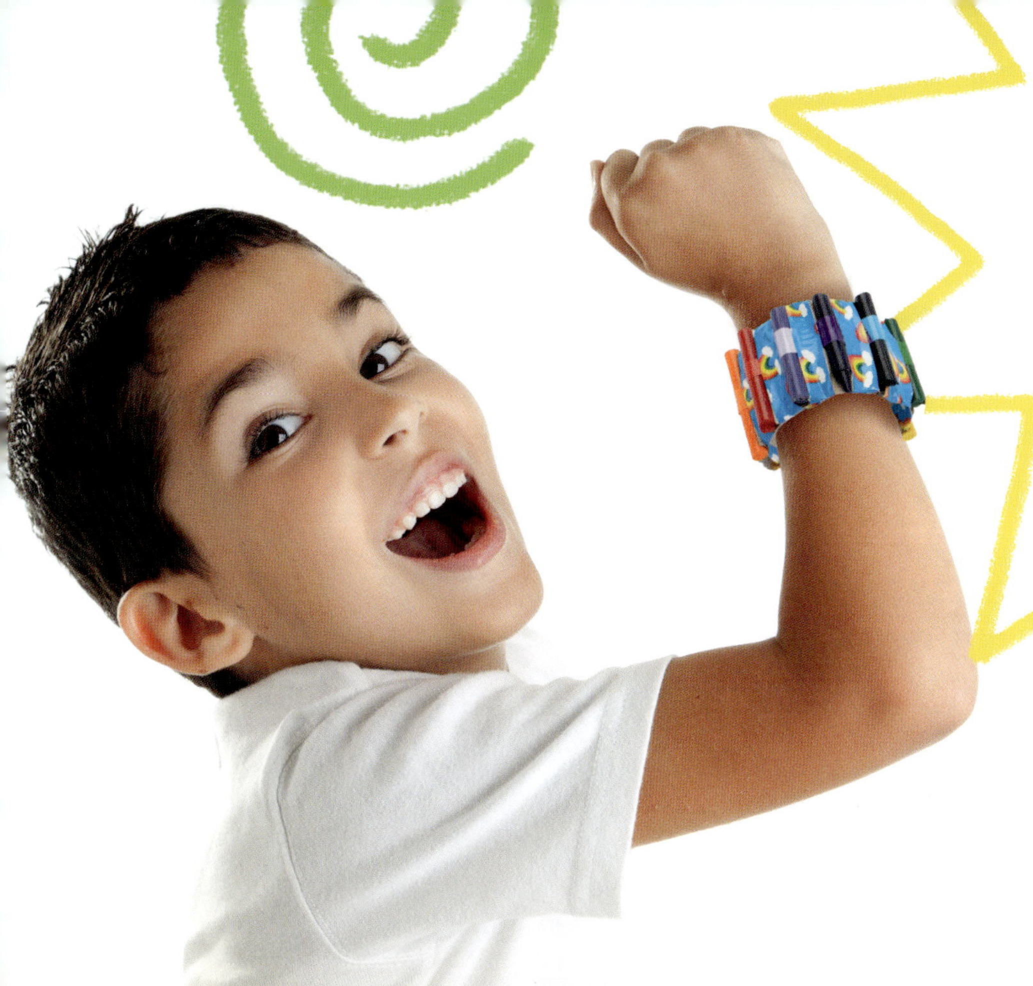

Problem-Solve

Every problem has more than one solution. Is your cardboard wristband too big? You could tape crayons inside it to take up space. Or you could turn the wristband into a headband!

Your Turn!

Could you use cardboard to make a hat or slippers?

How might you turn crayons into earrings or a necklace?

Could duct tape be shaped into a belt or woven into a bag?

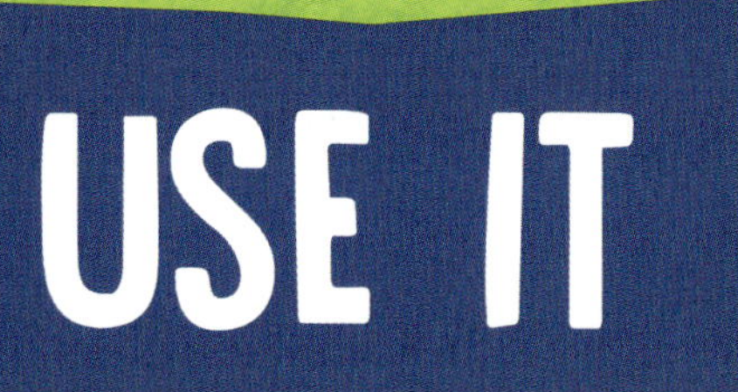

USE IT

Think of an item you need. Then **design** it! Cardboard, crayons, and duct tape provide many options for functional projects.

Rolls of empty duct tape can be stacked into a structure.

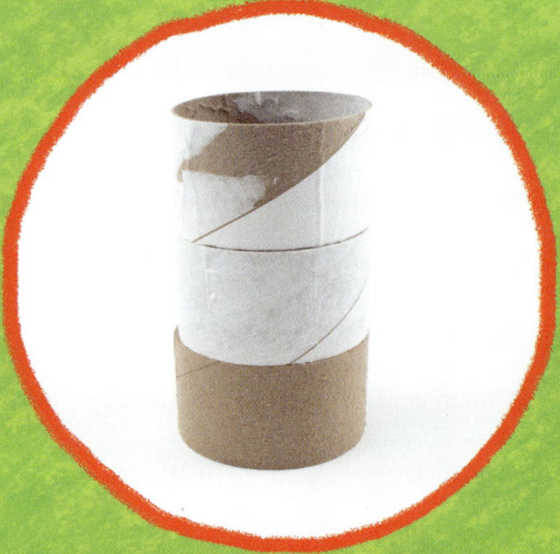

Laying down duct tape with the sticky side out creates a surface for sticking decorations.

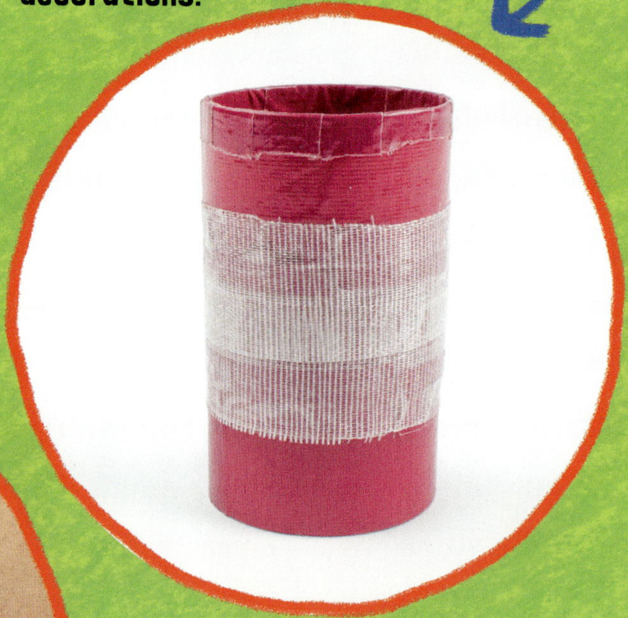

Shaved crayon bits look like confetti! Roll a sticky surface over these bits for a burst of color.

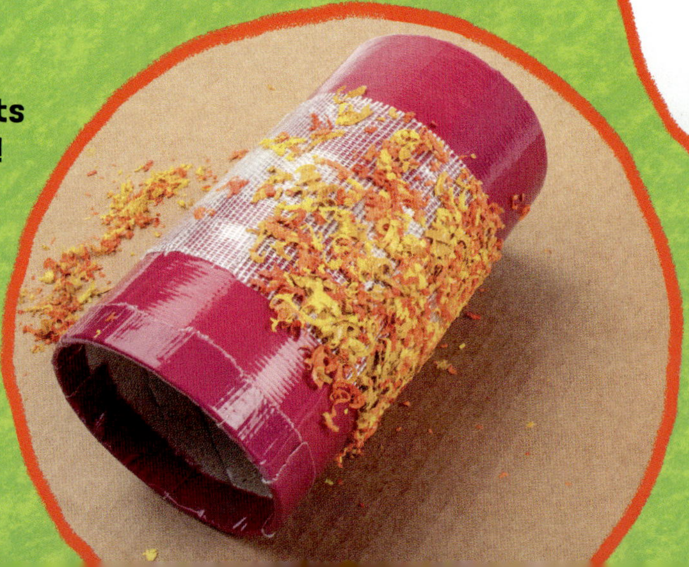

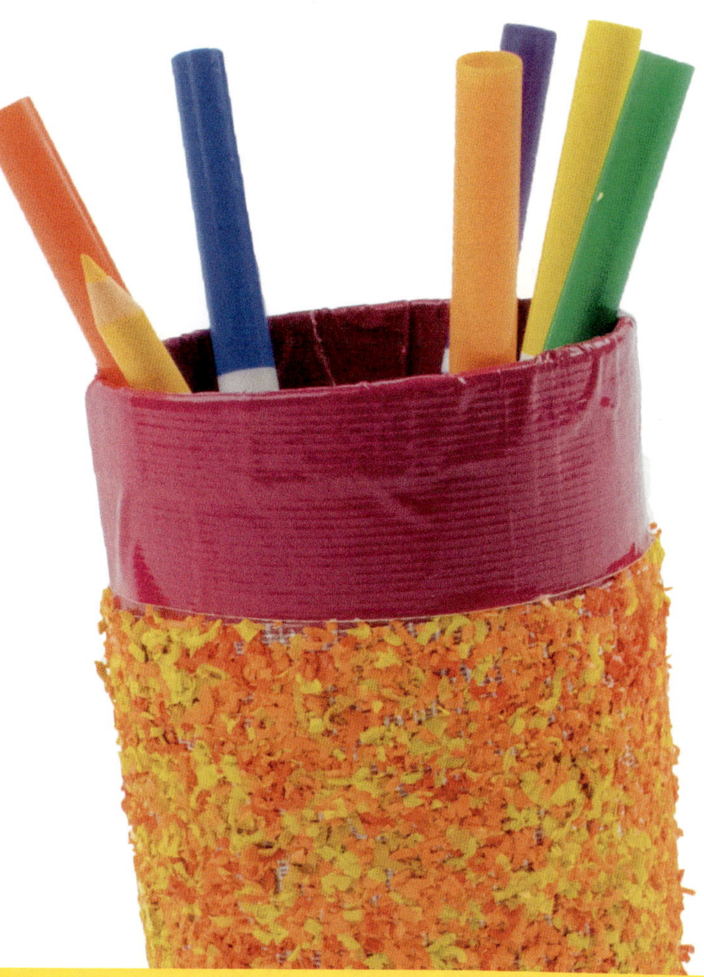

Get Inspired

Think about items you use every day, such as coin pouches or book bags. Look at these functional items as you come up with your own designs.

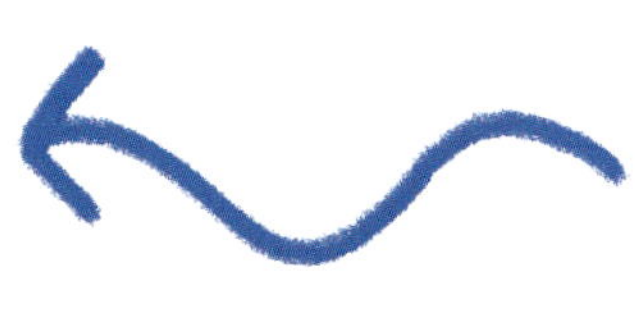

Now you have a homemade holder for pencils, markers, rulers, and more!

Your Turn!

Could you turn a cardboard box into a storage bin or a case for eyeglasses?

How could crayons be used to make handles, levers, or buckles?

How might you turn duct tape into a lunch bag or key chain?

BUILD IT

Engineers use all kinds of materials to build. What do you want to construct? Can you do it using only cardboard, crayons, and duct tape?

Think about the properties of your materials. Crayons are made of wax. Wax floats! Crayons can be used to create the base of a boat.

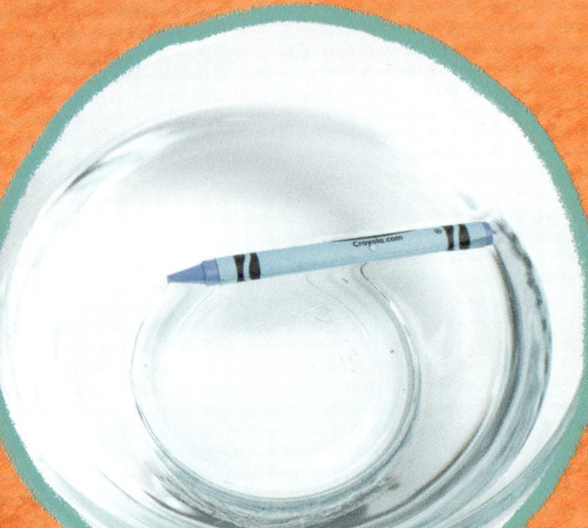

Crayons can be connected into a raft with duct tape. Duct tape is water-repellent, so it won't fall off in the water.

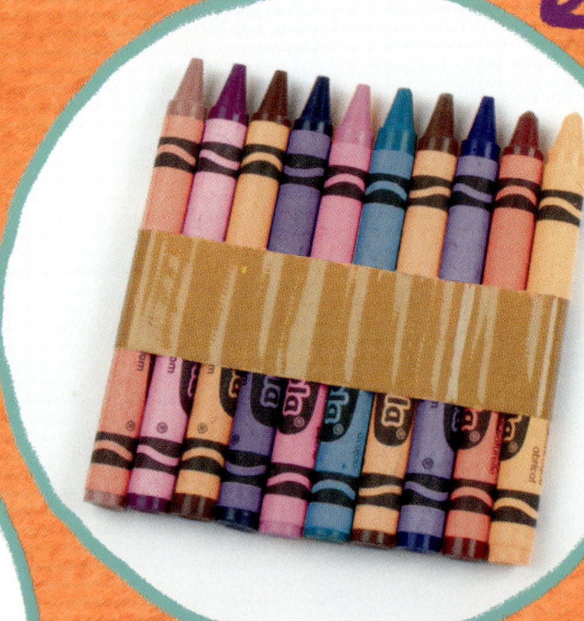

Duct tape fabric makes a great sail on a small boat!

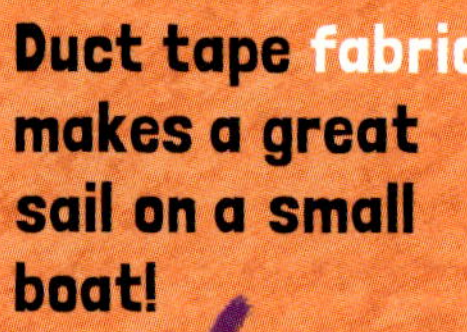

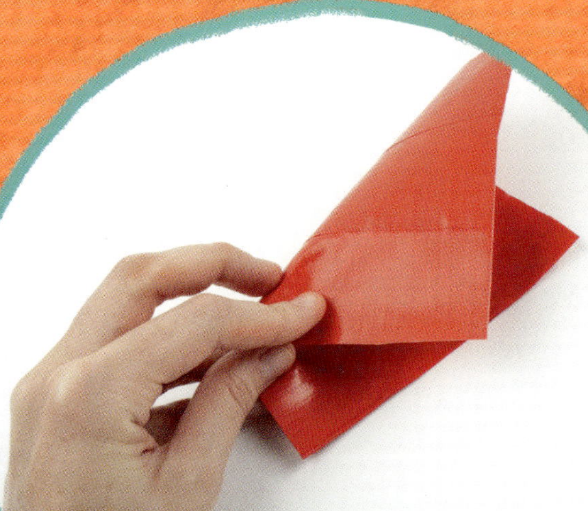

Bits of cardboard can hold up a crayon mast without weighing a boat down. Covered in duct tape, the cardboard becomes water-repellent.

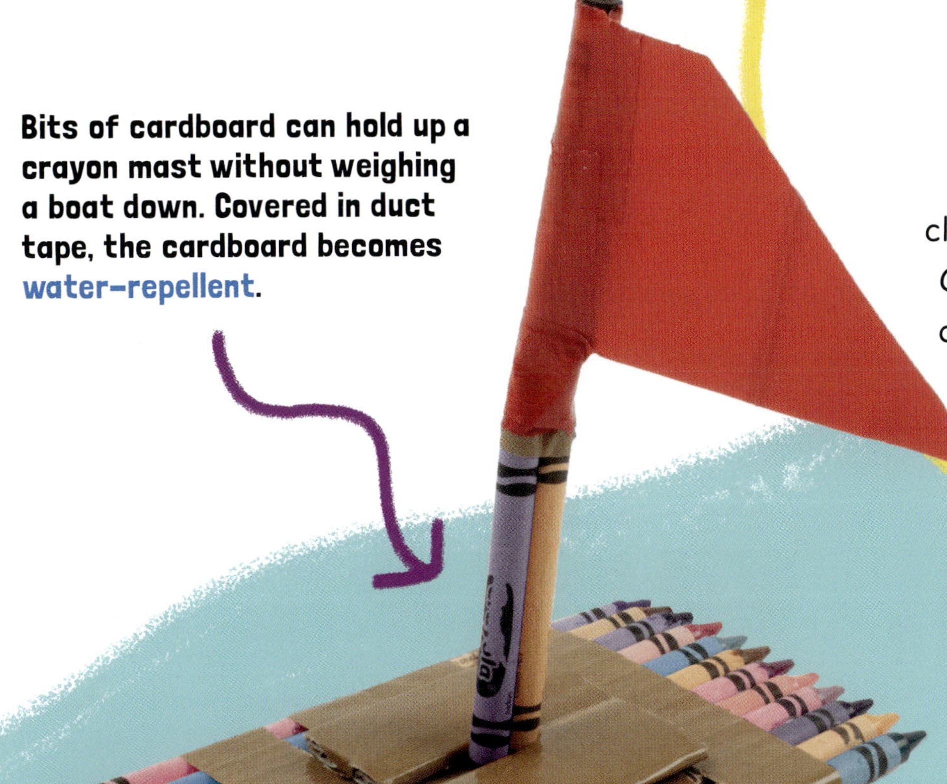

Collaborate

Don't be afraid to ask a friend or classmate for help with your project. Other makers might have ideas you didn't think of! They can also lend a hand during construction.

Your Turn!

How else could you construct with cardboard? Could it be rolled up or folded?

What else could you engineer with crayons? A tower? A fence?

Could duct tape alone be used to create the base of a boat?

GIFT IT

Is a holiday or birthday coming up? Do you want to surprise a friend or family member just for fun? You can make all kinds of homemade gifts using cardboard, crayons, and duct tape.

Corrugated cardboard can be used as decoration! It can look like feathers, scales, or other patterns.

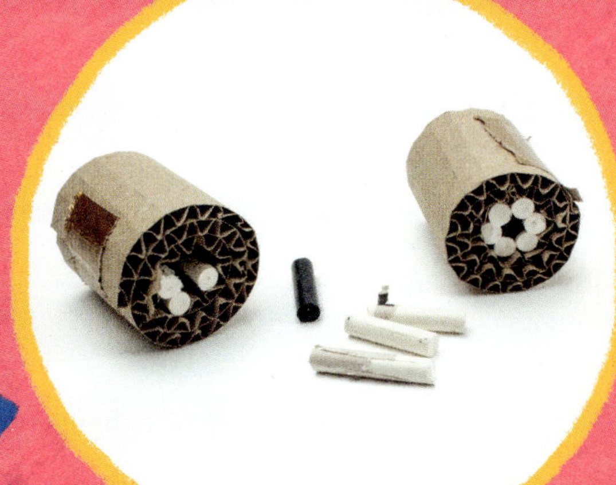

Cardboard duct-tape rings can become the outline of a face, body, sun, and more.

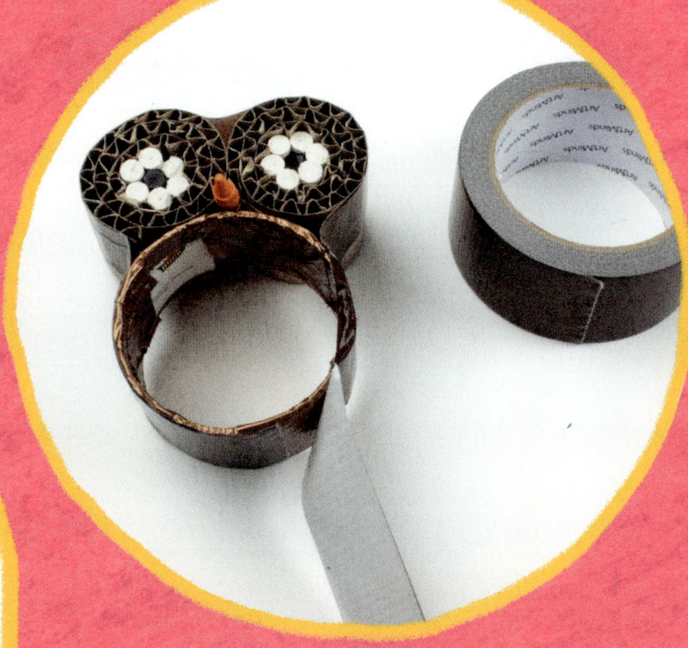

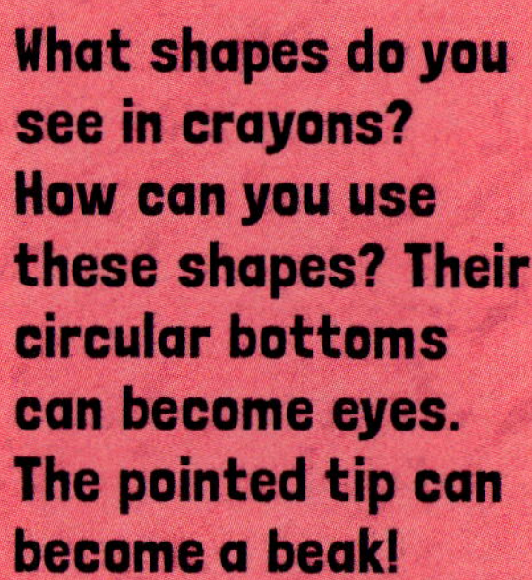

What shapes do you see in crayons? How can you use these shapes? Their circular bottoms can become eyes. The pointed tip can become a beak!

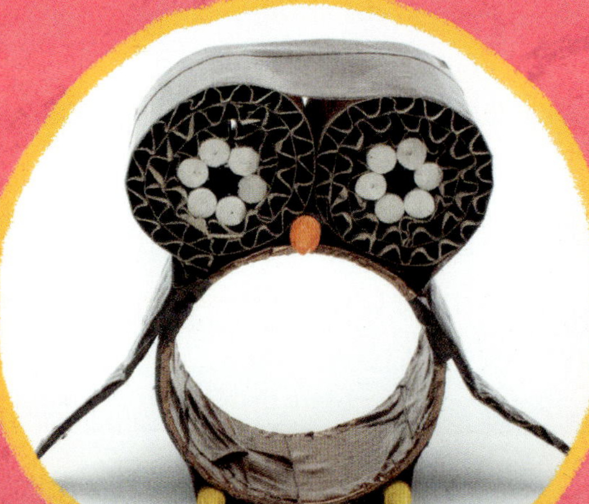

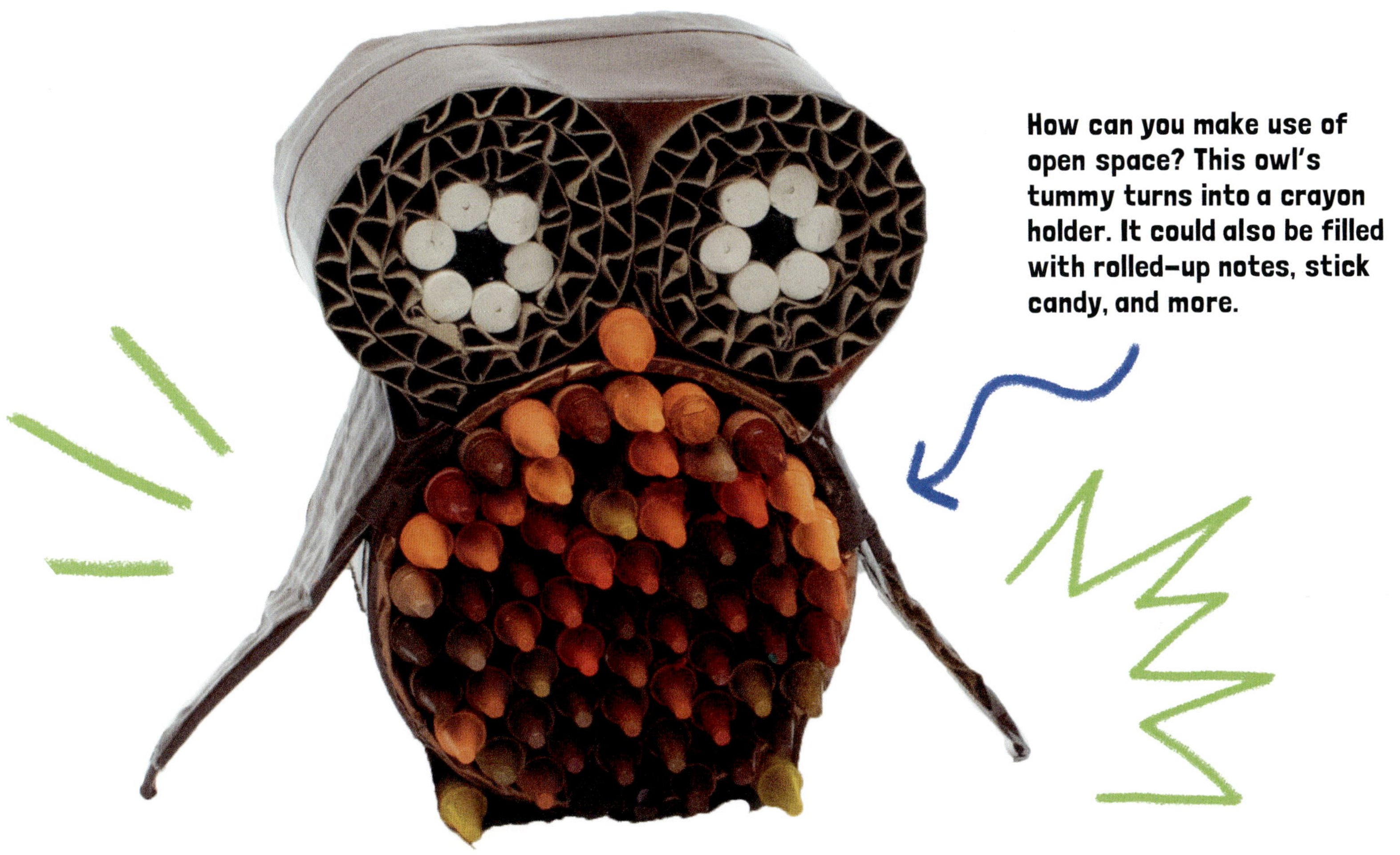

How can you make use of open space? This owl's tummy turns into a crayon holder. It could also be filled with rolled-up notes, stick candy, and more.

Your Turn!

How would you use cardboard to make a picture frame or pop-up card?

How else could you package crayons to give as a gift?

Could duct tape be shaped into a bow tie? Folded into a flower?

PLAY WITH IT

Looking for something fun to do? Use cardboard, crayons, and duct tape to create your own toys and games!

Thick cardboard can be tough to fold. Scoring can help. Use a craft knife to cut partway through a sheet of cardboard. The cardboard should easily fold at the line you cut.

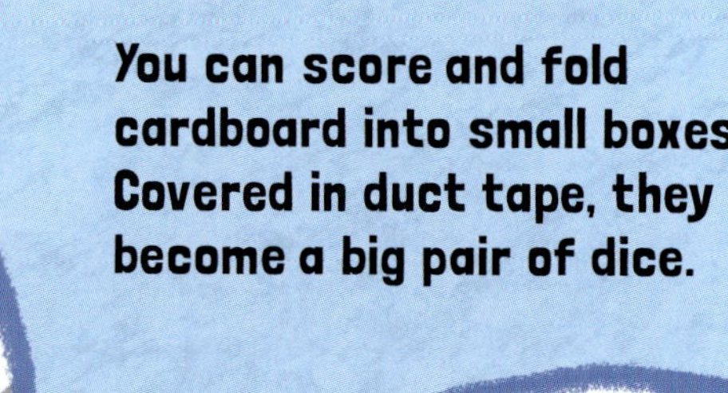

You can score and fold cardboard into small boxes. Covered in duct tape, they become a big pair of dice.

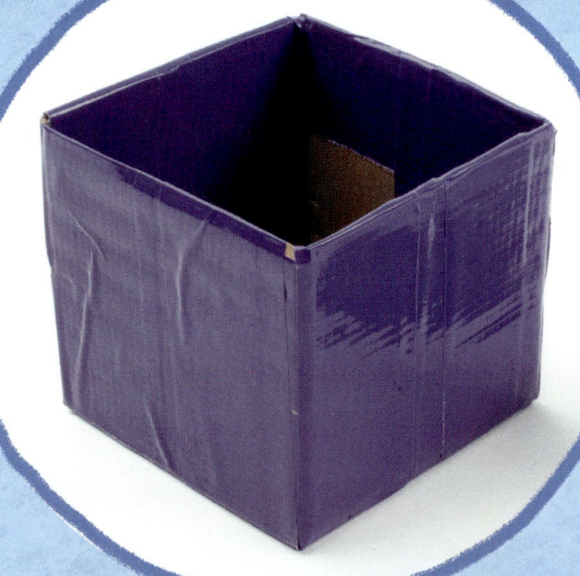

A sharpened pencil can be a tool to poke holes. But work carefully!

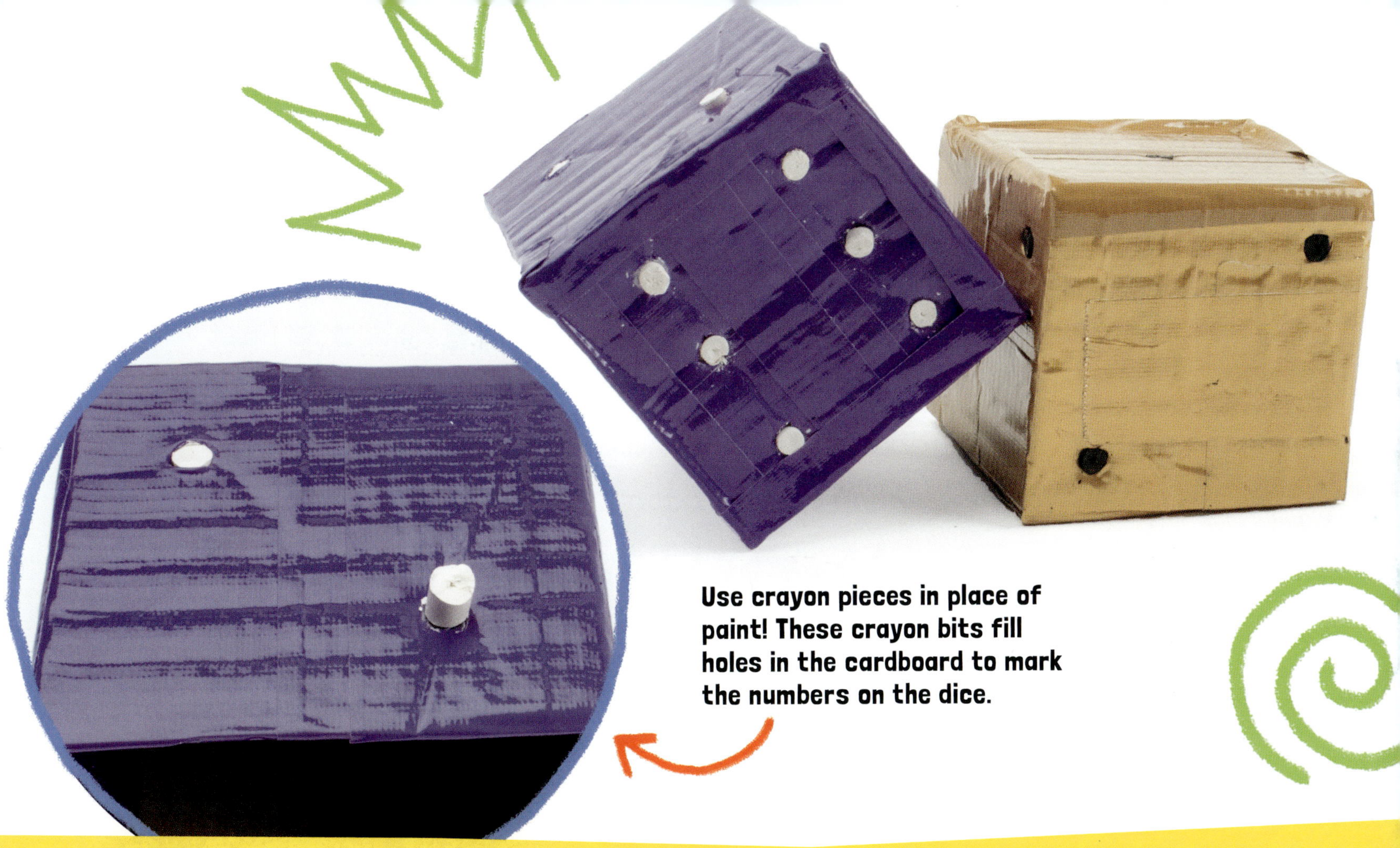

Use crayon pieces in place of paint! These crayon bits fill holes in the cardboard to mark the numbers on the dice.

Your Turn!

How might you turn cardboard into a board game or stacking game?

Could you turn crayons into game pieces or the border of a maze?

Could duct tape be woven into a basketball net or rolled up into a ball?

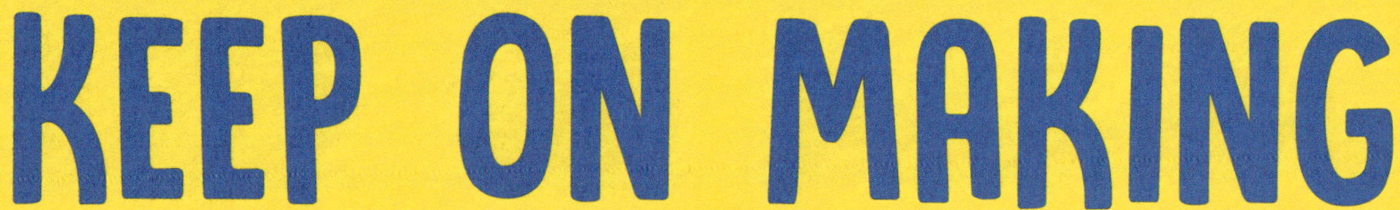

KEEP ON MAKING

Your cardboard, crayon, and duct tape projects may look complete, but don't close your makerspace toolbox yet. Think about what would make these projects even better. What would you do differently if you made each one again? What would happen if you used different methods or added another material?

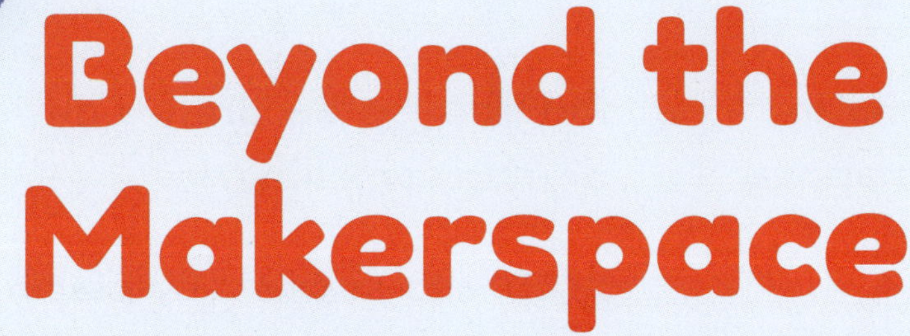

Beyond the Makerspace

You can use your makerspace toolbox beyond the makerspace! You might use it to accomplish everyday tasks, such as doing the dishes or taking your pet for a walk. But makers use the same toolbox to do big things. One day, these tools could help create a new type of clothing or allow humans to live in space. Turn your world into a makerspace! What problems could you solve?

GLOSSARY

accessory – a piece of jewelry or clothing that makes an outfit appear more complete.

collaboration – the act of working with others.

corrugated – having a wavy surface made of many folds.

design – to plan how something will appear or work. A design is a sketch or outline of something that will be made.

detail – a small part of something.

fabric – woven material or cloth.

flexible – easy to move or bend.

mosaic – a decorative design made up of many small parts.

prop – to support by placing something under or against.

replica – an exact copy.

solution – an answer to, or a way to solve, a problem.

texture – what something feels like, such as rough, smooth, hard, or soft.

tornado – a strong windstorm, usually with a funnel-shaped cloud.

water-repellent – made so that water can't easily get in.